S0-CTX-155

This edition first published in the
United States by Larousse and Co. Inc. 1984
572 Fifth Avenue, New York, N.Y. 10036
© Brown Wells and Jacobs Limited
First published by The Hamlyn Publishing
Group Limited 1984

ISBN 0-88332-377-X

Printed by Tien Mah Printing Company Pte Ltd. Singapore.
Print Consultant Landmark. London.

Picture Rhymes

written by
Dorothy D Ward

illustrations by
Chrissie Wells

designed by
Graham Brown

Larousse & Co.

These little bears take the bus in to school.

They're very good bears — they obey every rule.

They walk with their mother to the bus stop each day

But never cross over till she says they may.

Then they climb on the bus and say hello

To all of the other bears that they know.

The driver is kind — they call him Pete.

He knows where to go, up and down every street.

At intersections Pete looks to his left and his right

And carefully stops when he sees a red light.

When he gets to the school, he pulls up without fuss —

Oh, it's lovely to travel to school in a bus!

Tim has a boat that he sails on the lake.

If it sails right across it, how long will it take?

It might take a day or an hour or a week,

Or even a year, if the boat doesn't leak!

But losing a boat is a terrible thing,

So Tim keeps tight hold of the end of the string.

Mary's poor dolly has broken her arm,

So Mary is sad and full of alarm.

"Don't cry," says Mommy. "She'll soon be all right."

And she mends the poor arm and ties it up tight.

"Oh, thank you!" says Mary. "What a kind thing to do!

Now my Christina will be good as new!"

It's Sally's sixth birthday and just for a treat

She has chosen the things that she likes best to eat.

There's ice cream and jelly and sandwiches too,

And a big birthday cake that is red, white and blue.

There are cookies, potato chips, candy and pop,

And some little bears just don't know when to stop!

Sally has had lots of presents, of course —

A doll and a doll house, a black rocking horse,

A pretty pink dress and a puppet on strings,

And ever so many more beautiful things.

But what she likes best of them all is — just look!

A lovely, fat, red-covered Fairy Tale Book!

It's holiday time and what fun it will be

For everyone's come down to stay by the sea.

Grandma and Grandpa bear sit in their chairs

And Dad's gone to swim with the littlest bears.

Bobby is splashing around — watch that wave!

"Look Mommy!" he calls. "Don't you think that I'm brave?"

All of the bears have found something to do.

It's Monkey-in-the-Middle for Mark, Sam and Sue.

Billy is building a fort in the sand,

With his bucket and shovel he makes it look grand.

Mary and John play with bat and with ball —

Only lazy Christina does nothing at all!

Three little bears like to play in the sun,

They all bring their toys and are having such fun!

Sue has her bike, it is shiny and new,

To turn the wheels round she must push with her shoe.

Poor Sammy's not happy and can you see why?

His kite is escaping way up to the sky!

Run quickly and catch it — it's not far away.

And then you can fly it another fine day.

Peter is lucky, with two of his toys,

Balloons are quiet, but planes make a noise.

There are butterflies, green grass and leaves on the tree.

And Mommy will soon call them all home for tea.

On Friday the market is held in the square,

The stalls are put up and the bears are all there.

Lucy and Katy are feeling quite proud

As they help Mommy carry her bags through the crowd.

They buy eggs and some fish and a beautiful jug

And Mommy has promised them each a new mug.

One mug is blue and the other is pink.

Which mug belongs to which bear, do you think?

Lucy likes pink and her sister likes blue!

Mommy buys socks and new cardigans, too.

"We do like the market," the little bears say.

"We're glad every week brings a new market day!"

Miss Ursula teaches the bears how to dance,

They curtsy and bow, they fall back and advance.

Each little girl wears her prettiest dress,

They have beautiful manners and don't make a mess!

The boy bears all make a very low bow.

"Hold hands," says Miss Ursula. "Start dancing now."

"Take a step to the left and a step to the right.

Now Bobby, don't hold your poor partner so tight!

Make a very big circle and dance all around.

Put your feet very carefully down on the ground.

Now a bow, now a curtsy — don't scramble, don't shriek!

And I'll see you all back here, same time next week."

The bears are all having a holiday treat.

They'll take a big basket with nice things to eat.

A walk in the country and then play by the brook

And find lovely flowers — they know where to look.

Sam takes his rod and some worms in a tin

And Mark has a net to catch tadpoles in.

The picnic bag's carried by Penny and Jane —

It won't weigh so much when they go home again!

There are cookies and apples and fruit juice to drink,

Sandwiches, cake, and some buns iced with pink.

They eat every scrap and then play in the sun

And then they walk home when the picnic is done.

While all of the big bears work hard at school,

The little ones go to the neighborhood pool.

They take swimming lessons, it's ever such fun,

They don't want to leave when their lessons are done.

Ben splashes and paddles and makes a big wave,

Betty floats nicely, she feels very brave.

Very soon they'll be able to swim like the others

Then they'll have races with their sisters and brothers.

Doing the breaststroke, the backstroke, even the crawl —

No one will be able to beat them at all.

Learning to swim really is so much fun,

For big bears, for little bears, for everyone!

When Simon woke up he was filled with delight —

He saw there'd been lots of thick snow in the night!

"Come on now!" he shouted. "Don't lie there in bed!

It's been snowing! Let's find the toboggan and sled!"

"You must have your breakfast," said Mommy. "Then go.

And bundle up warmly — it's cold in the snow!"

The snow was so soft, it was ever such fun

To slide down the hill in the cold winter sun.

The bears made a snowman with pipe and with scarf.

With his floppy old hat on he made them all laugh.

A good snowball fight is a wonderful game

And weren't they hungry when dinner time came!

Betty and Ben go to nursery together.

They don't want to miss it whatever the weather!

It's held in the hall at the end of the street —

That's the place where all of the littlest bears meet.

Mrs. Bruin's the teacher — she's kind as can be.

She reads books and tells stories and brings things to see.

She once brought a goldfish that swam to and fro

And opened its mouth like a very big "O".

The bears make birthday and Christmas cards, too,

With leaves and with flowers they stick on with glue.

There's paint and there's paper, there's cardboard and sand —

The little bears think that the nursery school's grand!

Granny and Grandpa don't live very far

So the bears often visit them — they go by car.

They drive through the country and up and down hill.

When Mommy drives fast it is really a thrill!

Grandpa's garden is pretty, with flowers and trees

And Grandma always has a treat for four o'clock tea.

Coming home in the evening, their Dad drives instead.

They watch the sun sinking, so lovely and red.

The birds in their nests settle down for the night,

And one star is shining, so high and so bright.

They play games on the way, they count cows and then sheep,

But when they get home — why, they're all fast asleep!